UNIVERSE
EARTH
CONCRETE PLANE
ABSTRACT PLANE
INDIVIDUAL
SOCIETY
EXTERIOR
INTERIOR

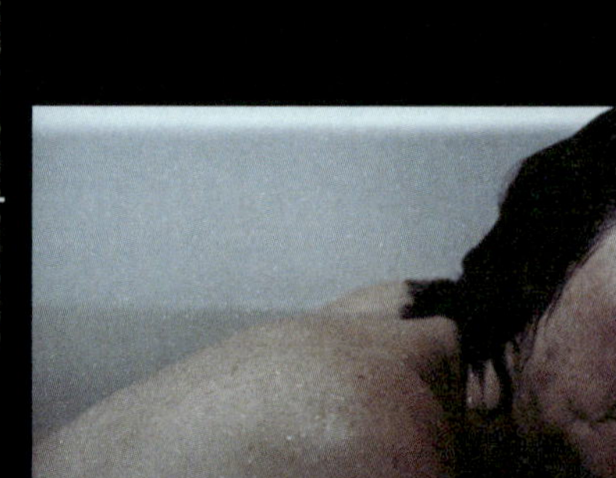

Carmo:
Where am I?
Where were you?

Irma:
Were you?
Where were you?

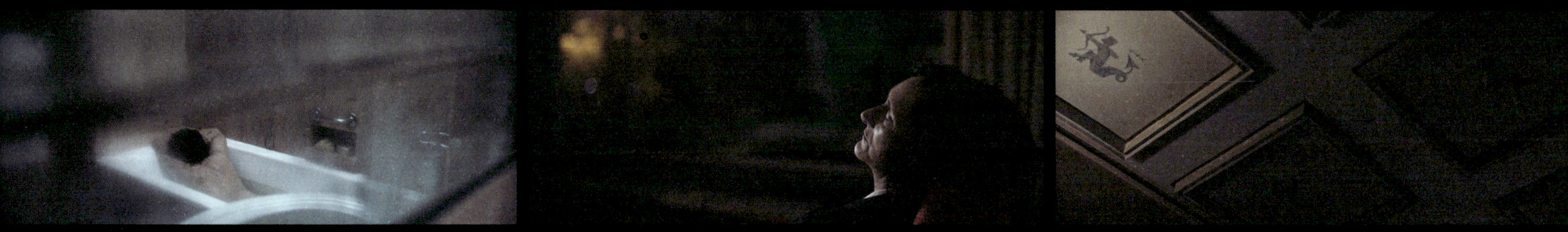

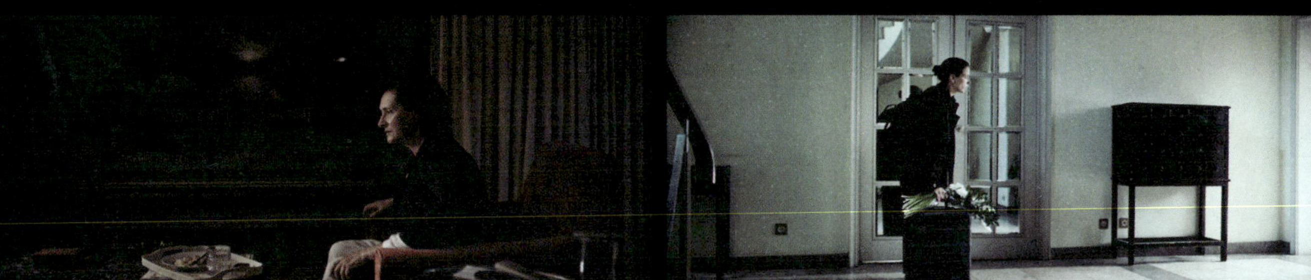

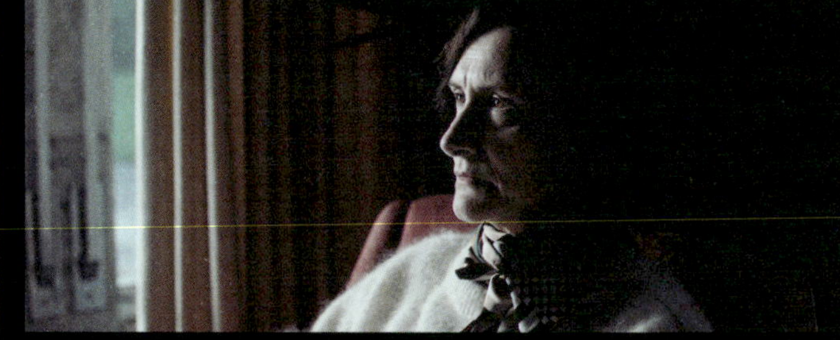

Carmo:
Have you been there long?

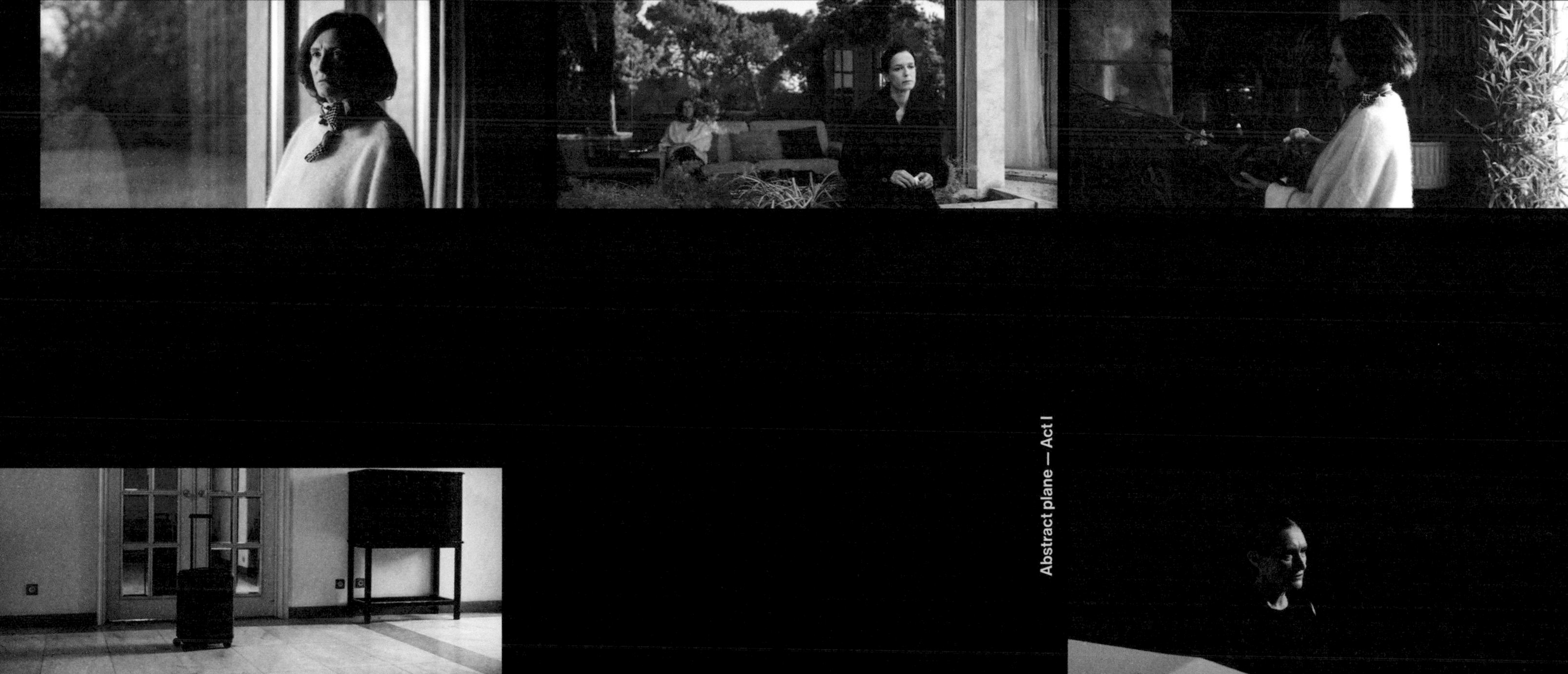

Abstract plane — Act I

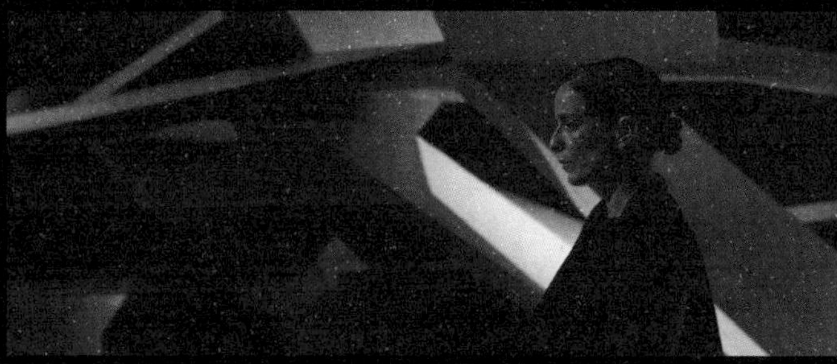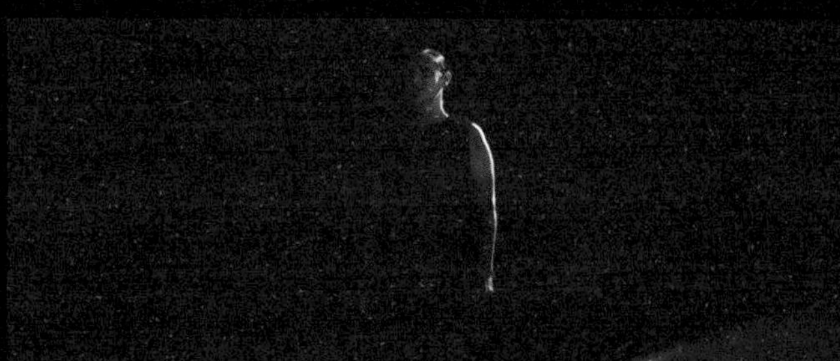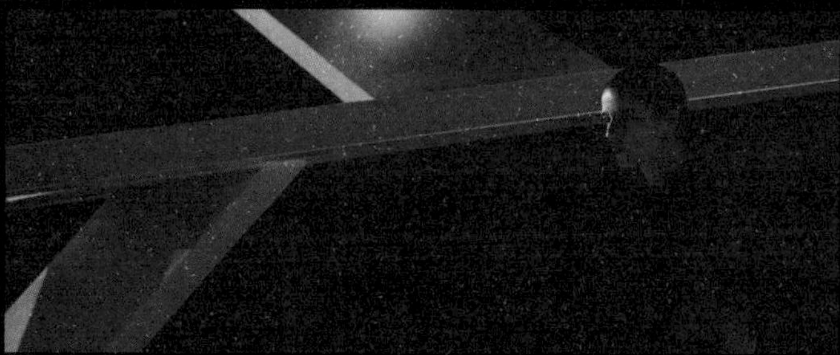

Carmo:
Life is split between the living who circulate, assert, and liberate themselves, and the corpses of permanence, that hold on to an acritical, familiar, and cautious existence. It's a trajectory that cannot be replicated, remade, or dominated, it resists classification and defies stereotypes. To remain means being spiritually exterminated.

Irma:
Our experience, condition, age and point of view redefine our memories. Our defense has always been justified by the notion that there is one way of being, a certain truth, or a conception of truth, which has guided many of the choices of different periods of history.

Carmo:
Certain American myths say that the first men lived inside their mother for some time, in the womb of the earth, so they would develop further, so they would mature. That children come from the depths of the earth, the caverns, the grottos, the crevices, but also from the seas, the springs, the creeks.
When dying, one hopes to reencounter Mother Earth.

Irma:
Myths don't explain reality, they merely affirm a certain image of the world without explanation. It's depoliticized discourse.

Carmo:
All things are possible. We're only limited by what we claim to be. I'm the world before the creation of the world. I am thought and desire.

Irma:
How can I know if I desire what I want? And how can I know the right word to name what I want? But what do I want? The ends are, by definition, visible at a distance, but they lose their concrete character when you come near them.

Carmo:
On the trail, we take control of things; in the aura, it takes control of us.

Irma:
The impossible is real now, this stems from knowledge. Reflection is a property of matter.
In a maze, an organism similar to an amoeba finds the most efficient way to food. It solved the puzzle, it stretches its body, so as to link to the food. The mold oscillates between being a single creature and a swarm: sometimes it's it, sometimes it's them. That's how I saw God: by gluing my eyes to the ocular lens of a microscope. The engine of creation exists in the infinitely small, in disorderly particles that come together and form stars.

Carmo:
A powerful gravitational force makes the Milky Way dance inside itself. Distant galaxies appear in fictional places. Non-places. Places of non-happenings. What do we see when we see what's not there?

Irma:
Boredom is a kind of insufficiency,
of inadequacy, lack of reality.

Carmo:
No one present in the dual and strange space.
No one present to give meaning to what
is happening.

Irma:
What is happening.

Carmo:
It's happening, but I'm not there.

Irma:
I'm not there.

Carmo:
I don't realize it, but it continues.

Irma:
It continues.

Carmo:
On an unconscious level, colonialism did not intend to be seen
by the indigenous people as a sweet and kind mother who protects
her child from a hostile environment. In that country, the children
taught one another never to smile, they taught each other to lift
their fists, like hammers.
How can you be indifferent to that war?
There were no walls that could offer protection.

Irma:
Progress is only a myth.
A world of destruction in science participates. Science participates
in the destruction of the world. I'm lost in the search for a utopian
peace. But where is my utopia?

Carmo:
The country burned at low flame and we-I also began to burn.
Of embarrassment.
Who are we in that moment when it is necessary to be another to
survive? On the one hand, the need for metamorphosis.
On the other, the panic of becoming another.
The threat of dissolution and chaos.

Irma:
Feeling love for someone
and being loved by someone...
is a way.

Carmo:
Maybe love is giving someone something you don't have, and may
I add, to someone who doesn't want it. I chose a path. Or I didn't.
It was the only one.

Irma:
If we do not believe in the future I–we a[m]re planning or in those
around us, it is possible that a meteorological phenomenon, such as
a storm, will bring us closer to what we want.

Carmo:
Here cohabitation precedes any
possible community, nation,
or neighborhood.

Irma:
In the morning, as soon as I open my eyes, I feel the desire not
to see... Will I be able to save myself if I'm able to blind myself?
If I fail to see those whose destruction, I am capable of participating in?

Carmo:
I dream of ruins. They are the most alive thing
there is. Only that which becomes ruins survives
its destruction.

Irma:
She liked to hear me laugh, but I've given her
the exact opposite. I don't laugh anymore. I cry.
I don't speak with her anymore. There's a heavy silence between us.
I don't feel my body float anymore. I leave it behind. And with my
own, hers.

Carmo:
An otherness that over time we came to dominate, explore and,
ultimately... The ivy, the moss, the wild radish sprouts from the
cracks in the stone. They are confused with a lizard, like a delirium
of life that is born from death. A preserved ruin is monstrous.
All construction is destructive.
The plant life that envelopes the stones is the earth's revenge.

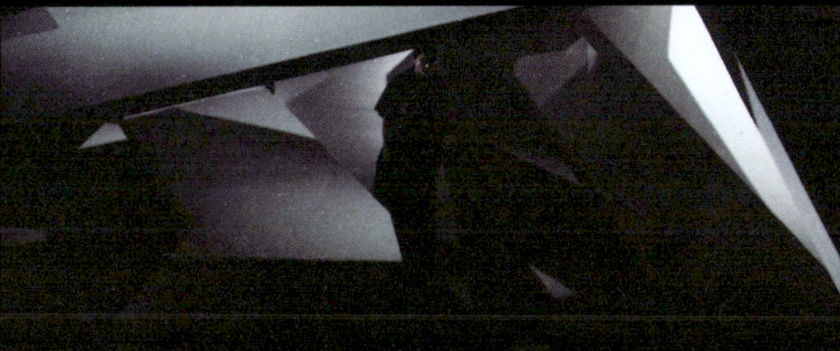
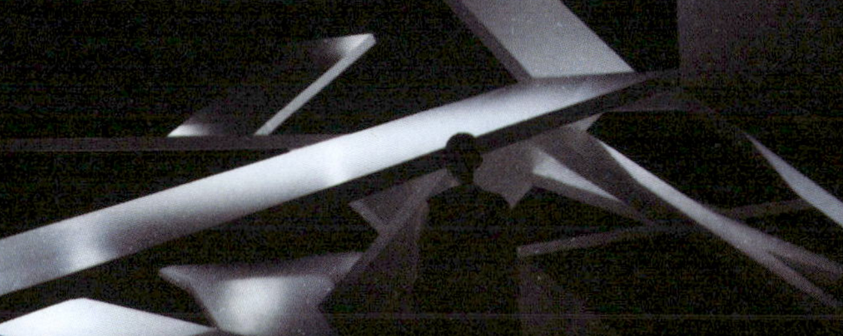
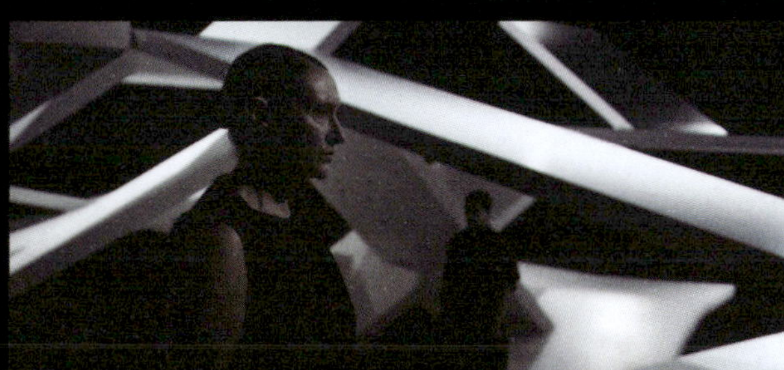
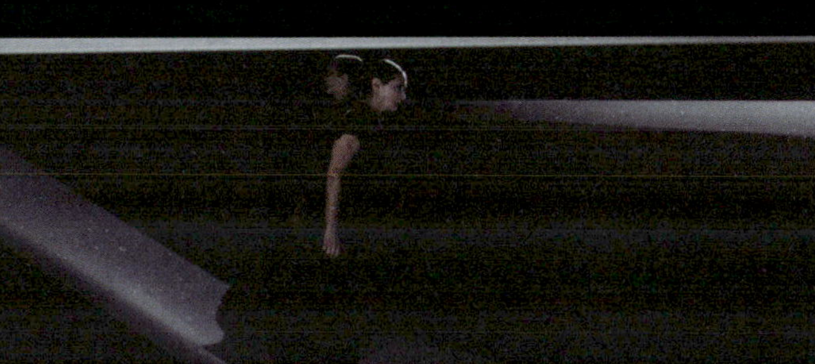

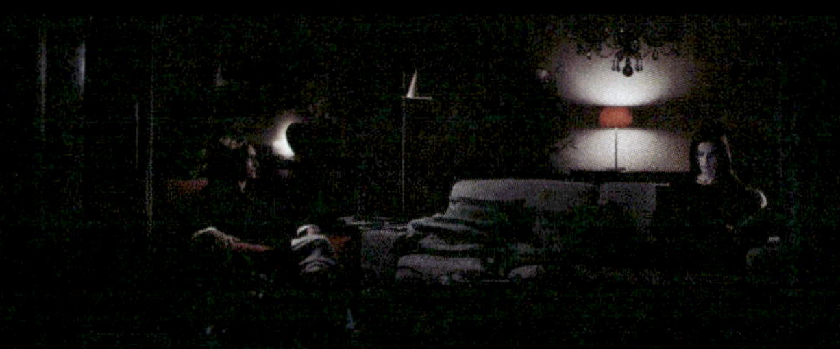

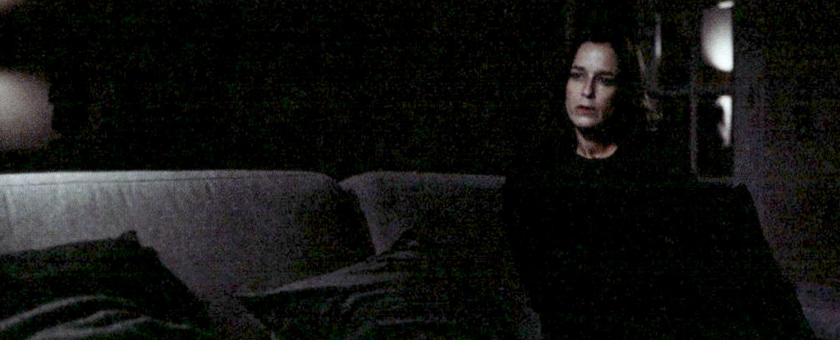
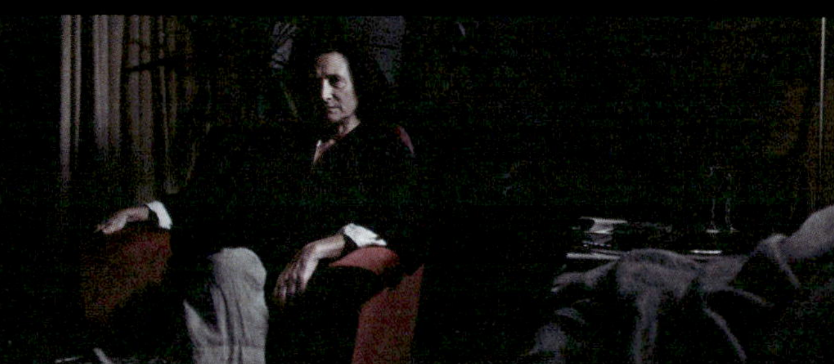

Carmo:
I see you smile, but you're
sad. And you're worried.

Carmo:
Try.

Carmo:
Sometimes people fool
themselves. You have to
remember to breathe.

Irma:
It's complicated, Carmo.

Irma:
Maybe I'm not the right
person for what I have to do.

Irma
Glória is away. I can help you
tomorrow. It's a way to rest.

Irma:
Why do you ask?
.
Irma:
No, Carmo. It's complicated.

Carmo:
You can run your own house.
And Luisa, is she doing well?

Carmo:
Because she's your friend.
I'd like to meet her.

Carmo:
I'd like to meet the person who's
going to stick around
and put up with you.

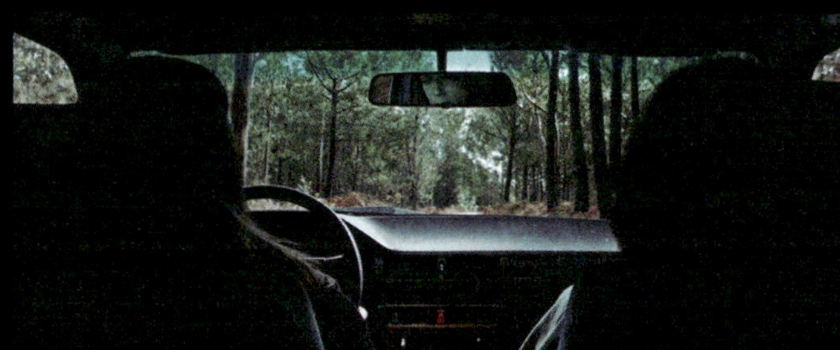

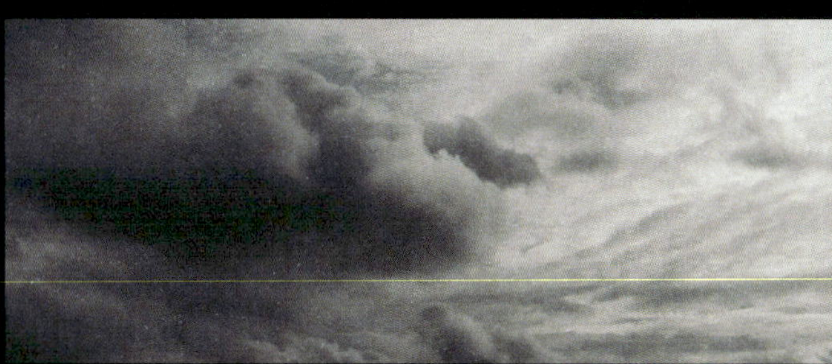

Carmo:
I'm going to bed. You do me more
harm than good.

I want to get out of the house.
See the sea. Will you take me?
One of these days.

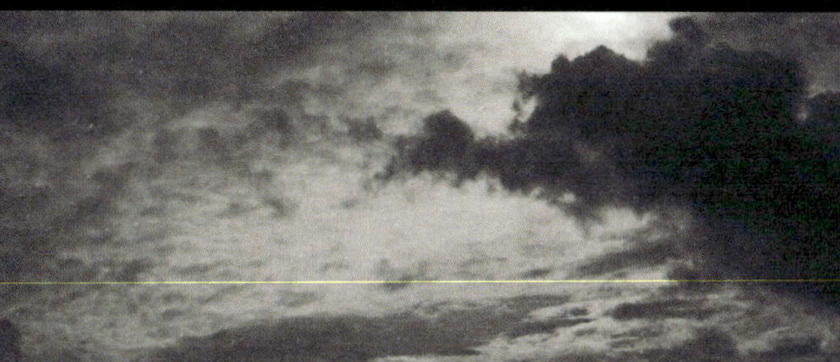
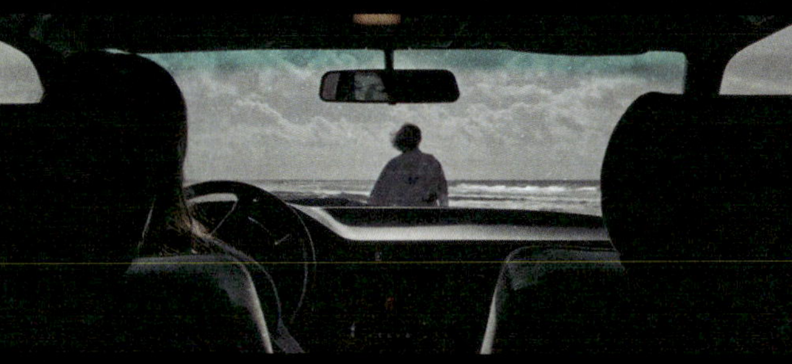

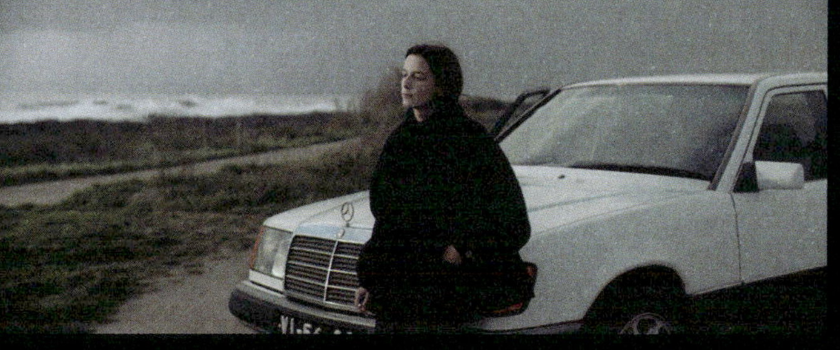 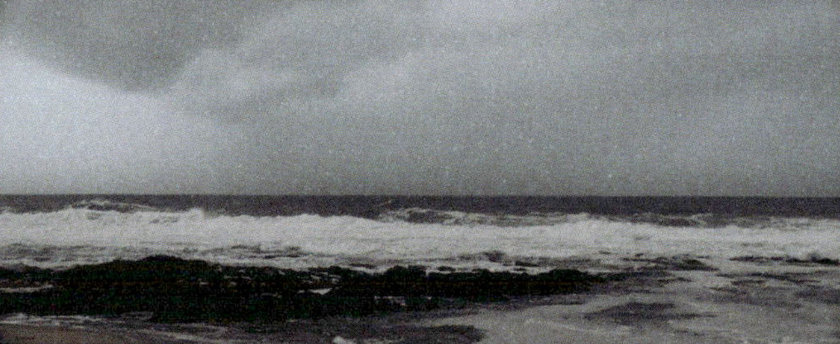 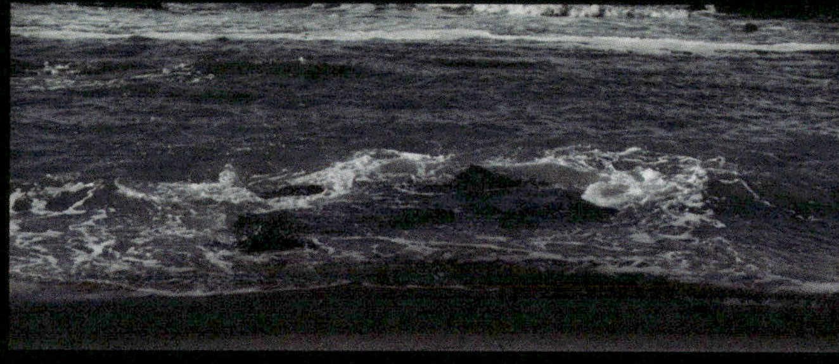

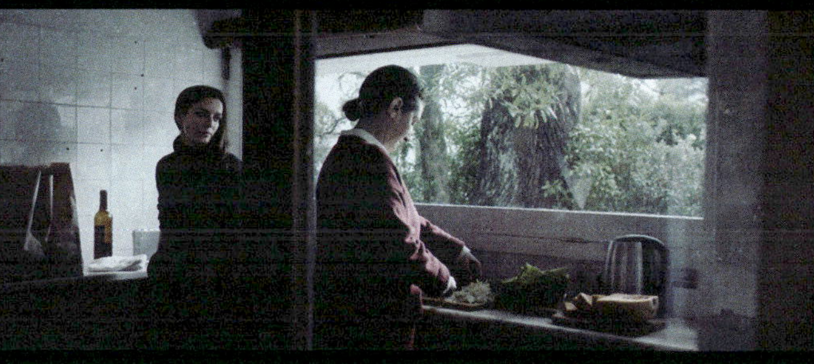 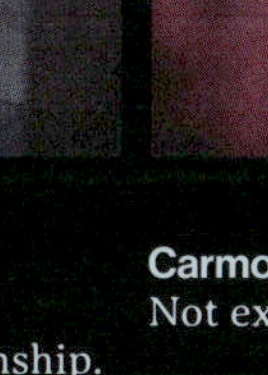 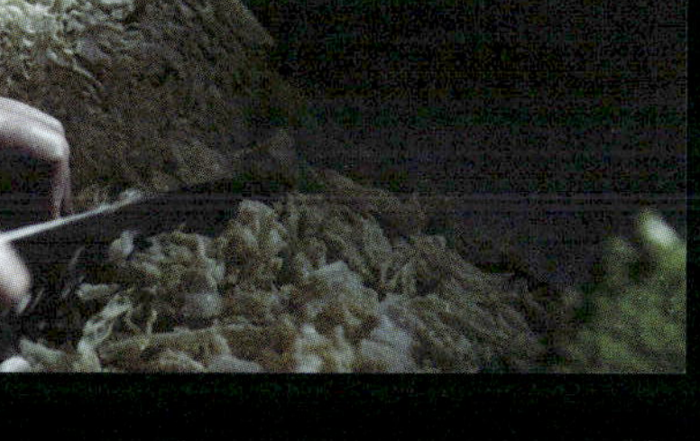 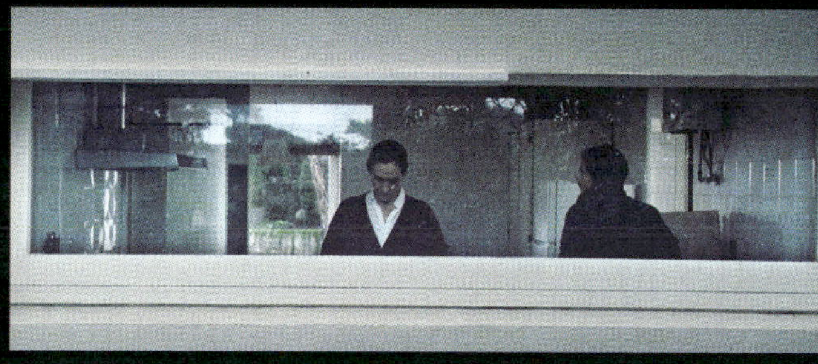

Carmo:
Move over! I'll do it.

Irma:
Age gives rank.
That was never our relationship.
Family doesn't have to be
sacrifice.

Carmo:
Not explicitly, that's true.

Irma:
Shaping another in my favor or
against me. I don't know if I'm
interested.
What about you?

Carmo:
What, me? You must think
I'm here forever. I refuse
to be that. Always available.

Irma:
Yeah, I know.
I've always heard you say that.

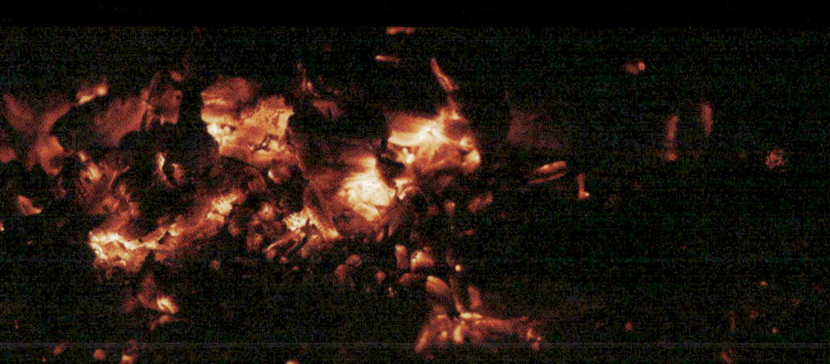 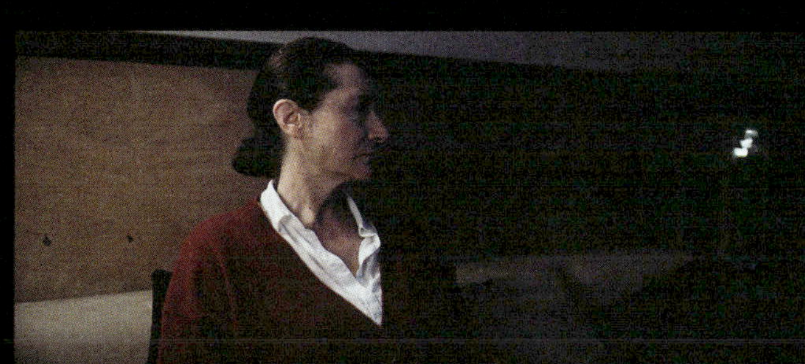 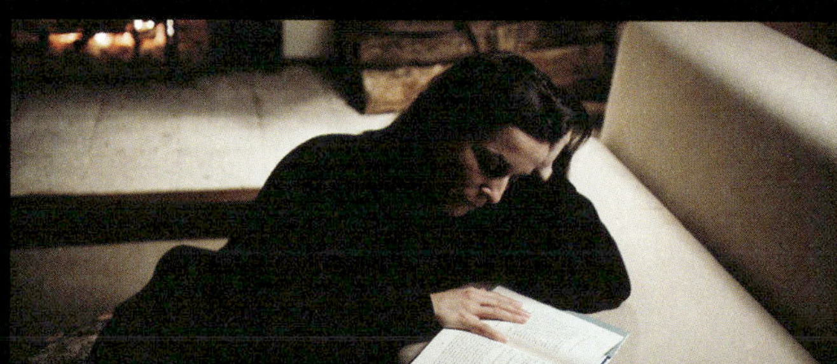

Antigone, Sophocles

Irma:
What is it? Well?

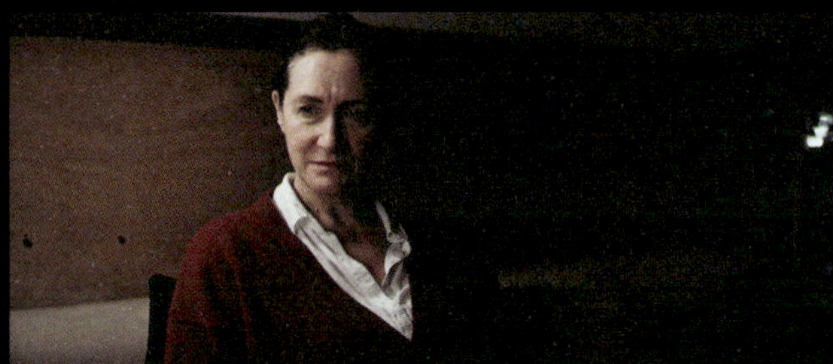

Carmo:
Tell me something. You must have things to tell me?

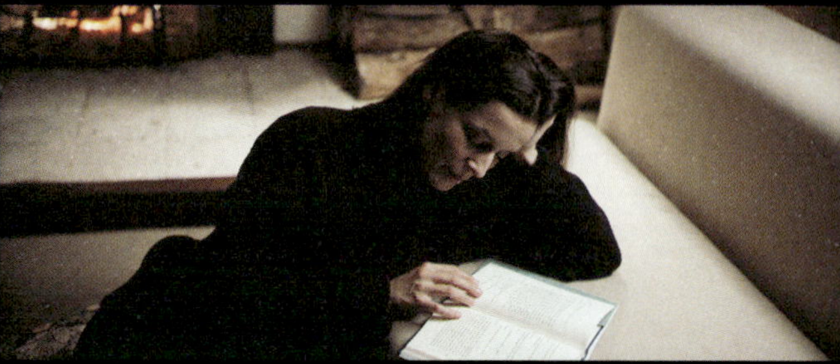

Irma:
Why don't you talk?

Irma:
Your life.
There's a lot I don't know.

Carmo:
About what?

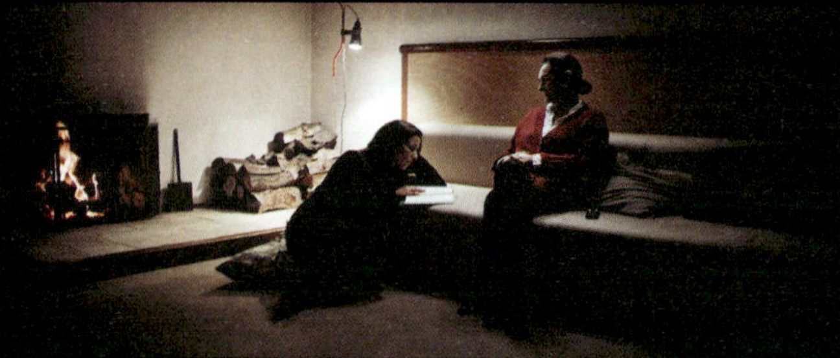

Carmo:
My life cannot be told in words, and I have a terrible, or selective memory.

Carmo:
I'm going.

Irma:
Right.
Aren't you going to bed?

Abstract plane — Act II

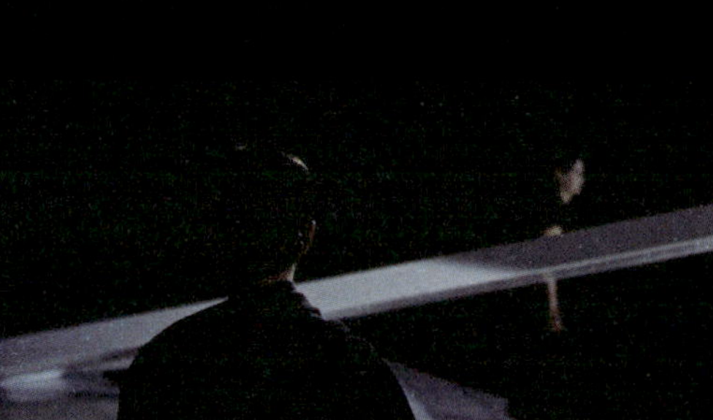

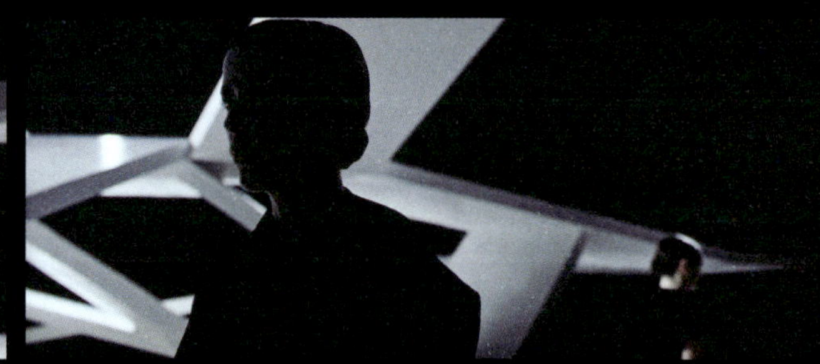

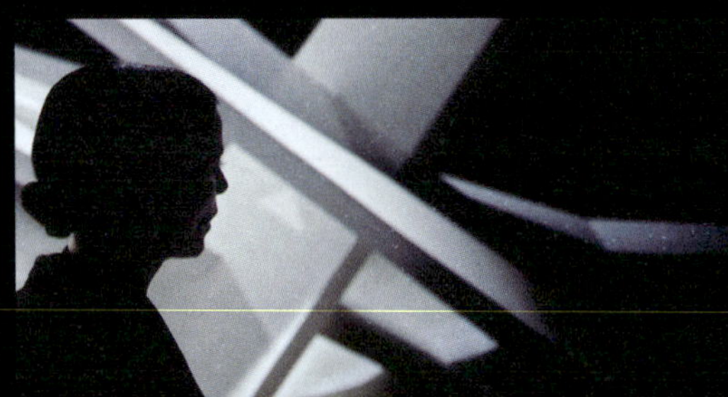

Irma:
Time is a movement that always moves forward.

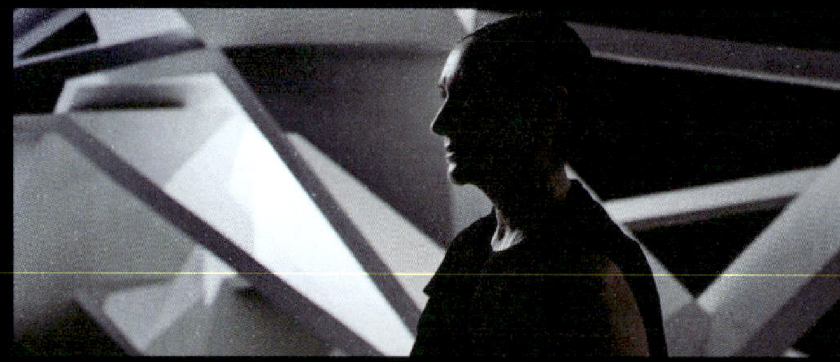

Carmo:
Snapshots of the past and projections of the future constitute the prosthetic of the present. Reality, in its immobility, does not contain history until the moment it's remembered.

Irma:
If light and time are inseparable, the absence of light is the absence of time. An alloy of ideas around an obscure center that drives and annihilates, a space-time where the future haunts us, where the past seeks to finally be, and for whom tomorrow seems like a prolonged blackout until civil war.

Carmo:
An ark has no belly; an ark does not swallow, doesn't devour, an ark is guided by open skies. However, the belly of this ark dissolves her, hurls her into a non-world for which it cries out. This ark is a womb, an abysmal womb. This ark is my womb, a matrix, and yet it expels. This ark: pregnant with as many dead, as with those living with death sentences.

Irma:
The universe is expanding, or something like that. Cosmic expansion is a form of antigravity, or something like that. The Planck wall prevents the origin from being seen due to a lack of light, or something like that. Perhaps it all started with a symmetry break, or something like that. The mystery of light against a dark background, or something like that. The twilight of a trauma against an illuminated background, or something like that.

Carmo:
Perhaps because the diffused background communicates the enigma of the never-ending. Perhaps because the universe is not total.
It's atonal.

Irma:
Our narratives are not only related to the rational assessment of the facts, but also with our emotional life.

Carmo:
The desire to prolong youth is not just a childish desire to eat one's own life and thus preserve it.

Irma:
Redoing is the categorical imperative of our times. He, Sisyphys, the rocks lover, who misinterpreted the meaning of Anthropocene, is now condemned to redo yesterday what he should have modified tomorrow. There is no high and low, no hierarchy of values, each form of existence is an object among the others.

Carmo:
There is snow on the palm trees of Borneo.

Irma:
If the same gesture is repeated, it is because he hasn't yet found a solution. Anguish, that turned into dull rage; he stumbled, halfway up the slope, lying on his back, he discovered the sky. And what a surprise it was then to see...

Carmo:
Our ecological crises were not hastened by man in an indiscriminate and generalized way. Anthropophagic sovereignty is done for the benefit of the dominant body and to the detriment of minority bodies. We are not exceptional.

Irma:
Why? One day the why sounds stronger and it's in that lassitude tinged with astonishment that everything begins. The distancing from the coherence of meaning reveals a system of fundamental intertwined illusions, that was once implicit and part of a way of being in the world and that now seems broken. In a universe suddenly deprived of illusions I feel foreign.

Carmo:
Behold the trees. Their trunks are rough. Behold the water. Behold the scent of grass and the stars. Behold the night. Shall I deny this world if I experience its strength and potency? And, yet all the science on this earth could never give me the certainty that I was not a stranger to it.

Irma:
A + B = C
It is a void without form or dimension.
A shadow you cannot see, but can feel with all your soul. Infinitely free. Now, knowing there was nothing to do, nothing to produce, only to remain uncreated in creation where meaning had drifted away.

Carmo:
Two possibilities. Become extinct or become another.

Irma:
It was necessary to think about this before.
From now on, asking for the impossible is the only possible way out.

Carmo:
Will we love our monsters?

Irma:
Monsters do not exist or are simply the result of a lack of attention to what we do.

Carmo:
Without separation, a relationship is truly impossible. Without the power of separation, any association becomes indistinguishable, as if it were impossible...

Irma:
As if it were impossible for the daughter to exist without the mother.

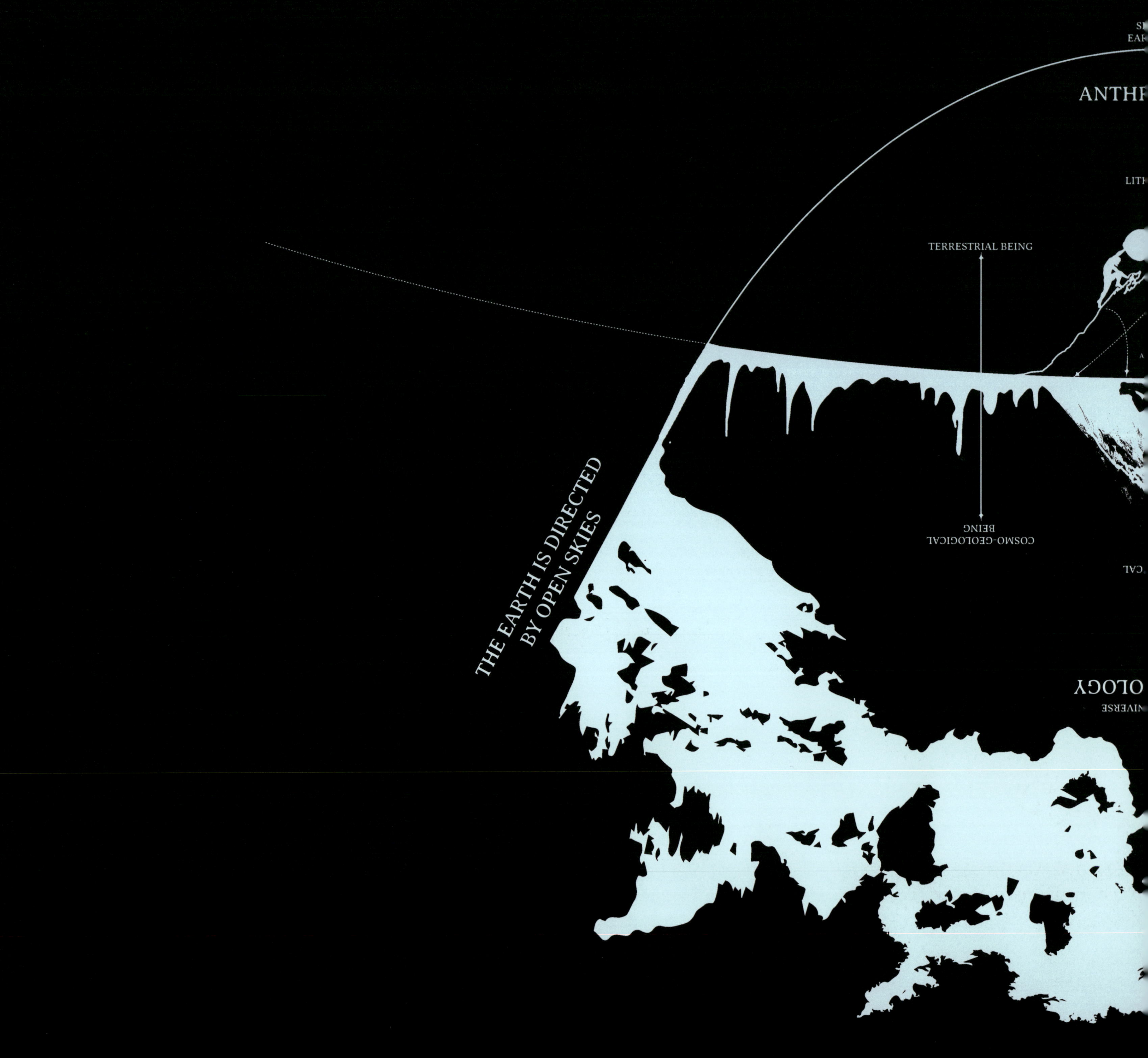
ANTHR
TERRESTRIAL BEING
COSMO-GEOLOGICAL BEING
THE EARTH IS DIRECTED BY OPEN SKIES
OLOGY

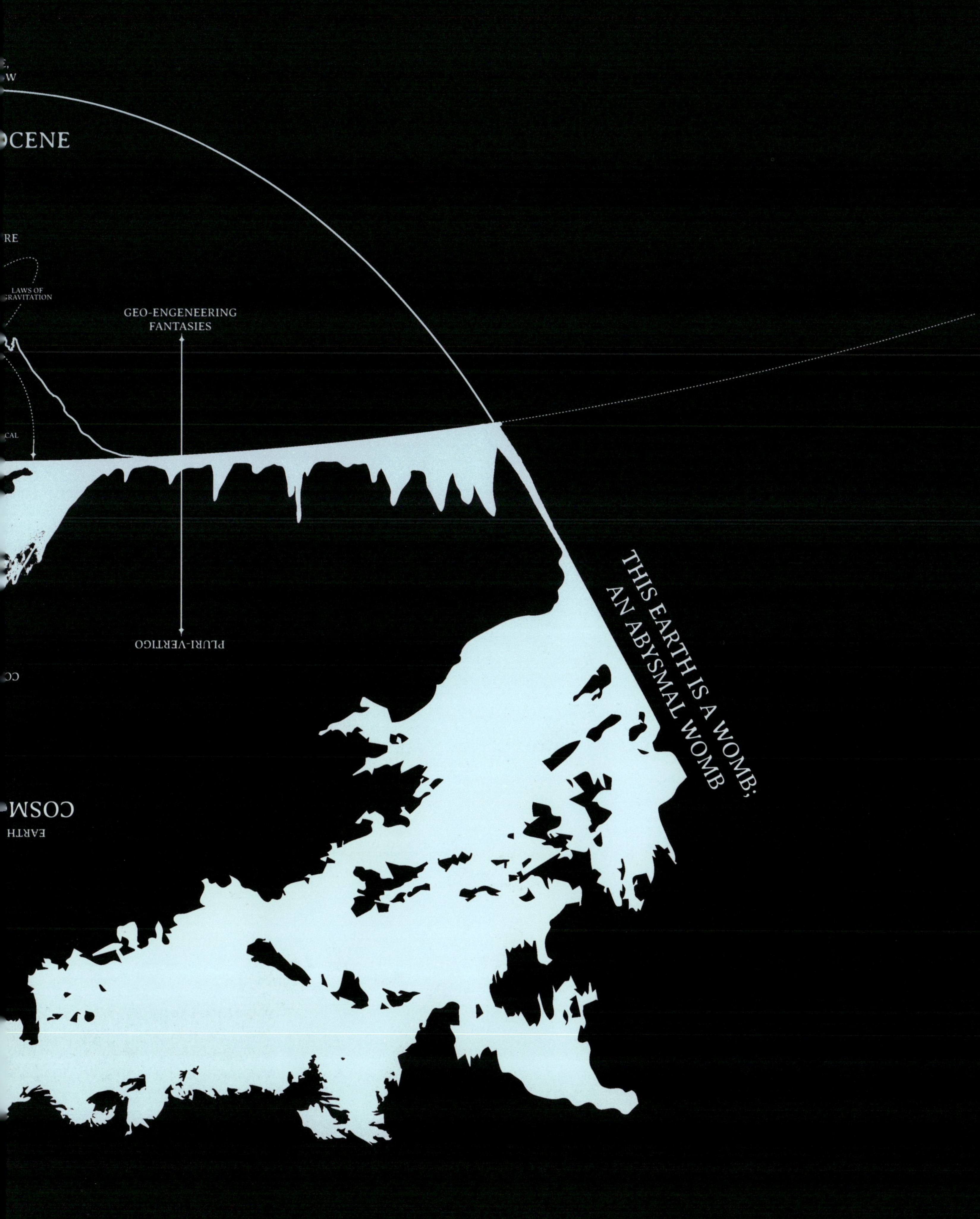
CENE
RE
LAWS OF GRAVITATION
GEO-ENGENEERING FANTASIES
CAL
PLURI-VERTIGO
COSM
EARTH
THIS EARTH IS A WOMB;
AN ABYSMAL WOMB

Carmo:
As if it were impossible be able to recognize that our destiny
depends on how we relate to the geological dimension of our being.
And with the stardust that forms us.

Irma:
Illusion, is a state of being,
grasped in the very process
of collapse.

Carmo:
Hence the melancholy.

Irma:
Take the pain out of your chest and put it in front of your eyes,
so we can see it and heal it.
That was never done.
When she dies, I will lose the place to go to.
Maybe at that moment I will allow myself to die too.

Carmo:
She went out to the blinding light. To the heat she carried like a
knife in her back. To step on the land of those, who when dying of
thirst, cut their veins and drink their own blood. At first the path
did not look like a path. Then, as strange as it might seem, there was
no doubt that a path passed through there. The paths had eyes and
mouths and arms and hunger. They were alive. They moved.

Irma:
Thousands of tribes and kingdoms pushed into the spaces between
lines on a map. Countries, identities. In fact, she was quite surprised
by the certainty that people have to have an identity. She didn't
have an identity. Maybe it was discontinuous. An agglomeration of
sensations and images.

Carmo:
Continuity is a demented idea.

Irma:
She said self-defense... Identity is
born by birth, but in the end, it is
not an inheritance from the past.

Carmo:
There the dead are alive. They sleep with
the living. The living carry the dead inside
themselves. They look for the dead. The
living are dead too. She lost her fear there.
She left it buried on the side of the road.
A dead man. Because of her.

Irma:
The feeling of the absurd, when
it is intended, in the first place,
to extract a rule of action,
it makes murder, at the
very least, indifferent and,
consequently, possible.

Carmo:
If you believe in nothing,
if nothing has a meaning,
and if we cannot assert any
worth, everything becomes
possible and everything
lacks importance.

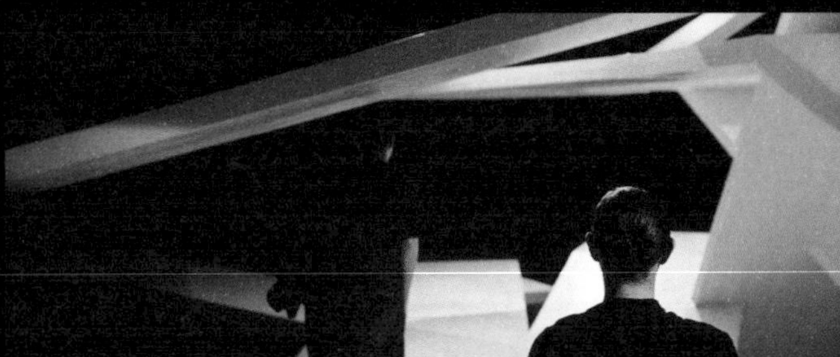
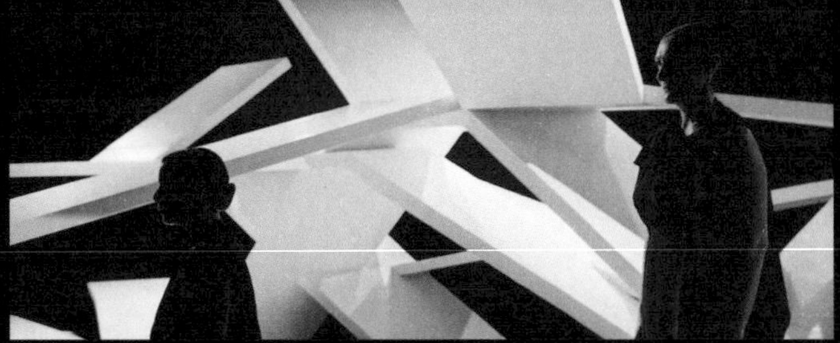
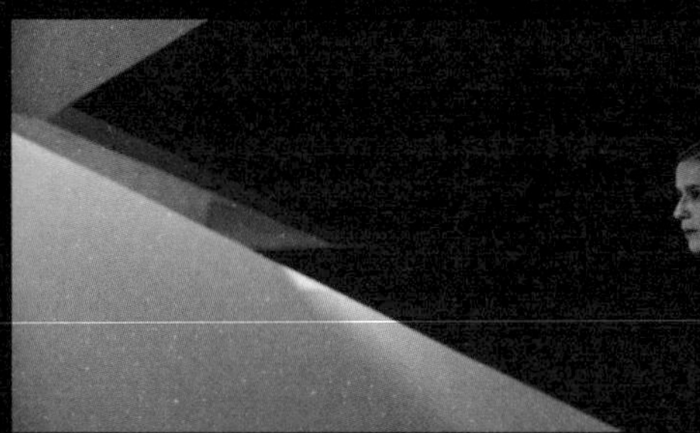

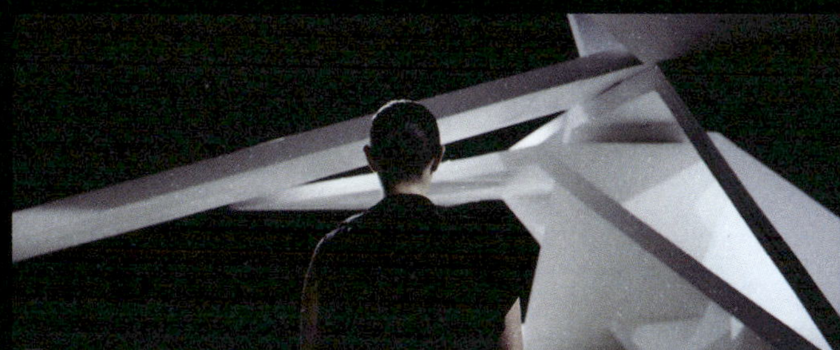

Concrete plane — Part II (cont.)

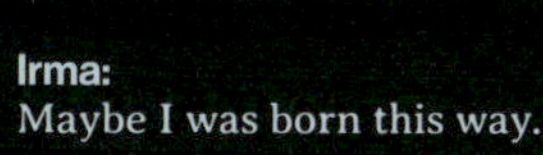

Irma:
I'm sorry.

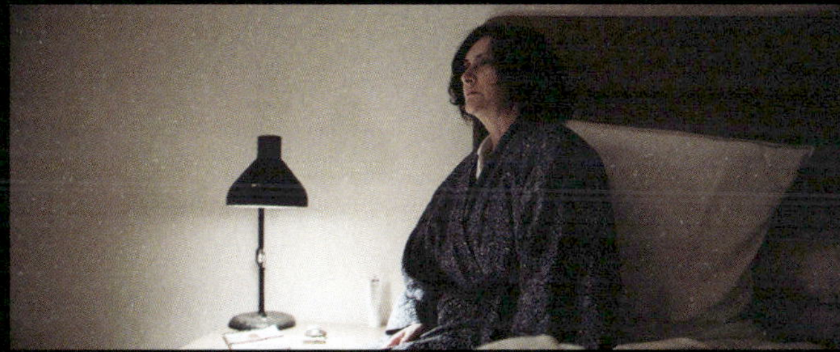
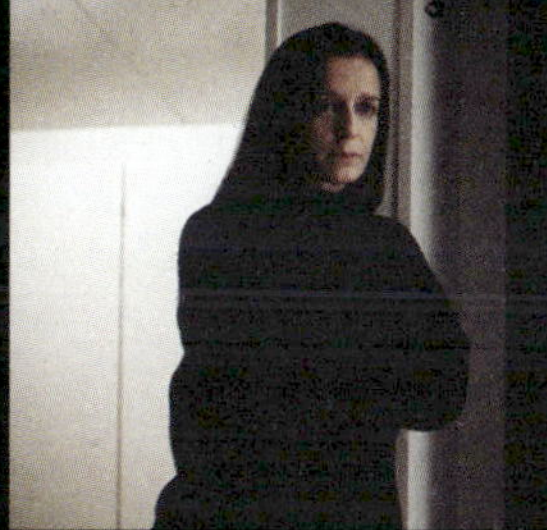

Antigone's Claim, Judith Butler

Carmo:
What do you know?
I don't care about words;
I care about actions! I fell.
That's it.

Irma:
You could have been hurt.

Irma:
So what?
You think that's fine?

Carmo:
I could have.

Carmo:
You're old. You know?

Carmo:
You're very serious,
very complicated.

Carmo:
Surely.

Carmo:
I have no doubt
about it.

Irma:
Maybe I was born this way.

Irma:
Is that what you think?

Irma:
One of us had to take care
of the other one.

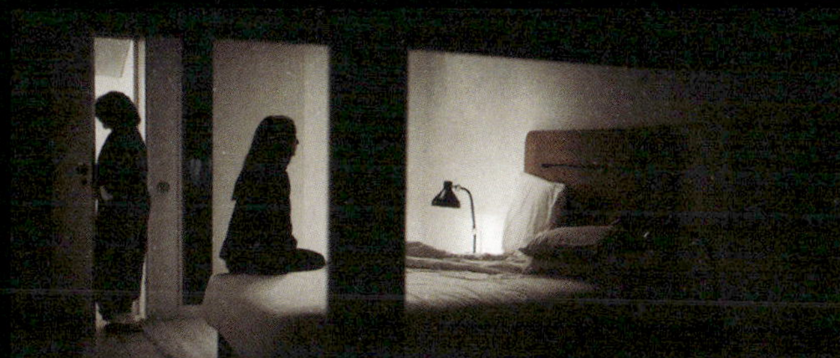
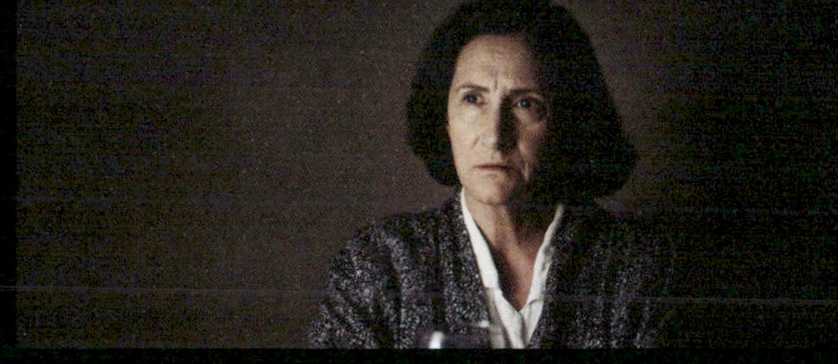

Carmo:
Must you insist!
And then comes the blame,
the apology, the counter-blame.
What a waste of time.

Carmo:
That's enough. It's a waste
of time, Irma. I'm not about
promoting this. What nerves.

Carmo:
That's what I intend to do.

Irma:
Carmo.

Irma:
Why don't you
take something?

Irma:
It seems that some things don't
bother you as much anymore.

Carmo:
It's not quite like that. The lack
of movement has never bothered
as much. And you were always
with me.

Irma:
I'm not even sure
where we have been.

Carmo:
And do you know now?

Irma:
Too much time spent
deconstructing you and
reconstructing you.

Carmo:
You're not making sense.
At least you know I didn't
let you grow up in an unsafe
environment. And that is no
small feat.

Irma:
Is that why you split up?

Carmo:
Men suit us well. No, it wasn't.
All my life I've been reprimanded for having a will of my own, for
being determined to live and always though...but unfortunately that
was not what happened.

Irma:
To the point of forgetting
the others. You were so young...

Carmo:
Yes...I was happy while I was
expecting you. I think it's still
like that. I'm happy while I'm
waiting for you. But then...

Irma:
How unpleasant.

Carmo:
What? We both came back without hesitation.

Irma:
I'm sorry that you came back,
but you did it for you.

Carmo:
Is it Irma, we master concepts,
which are nothing, but emotions
which are everything that's...

Irma:
About that time, I don't remember anything.

Carmo:
You weren't like this.

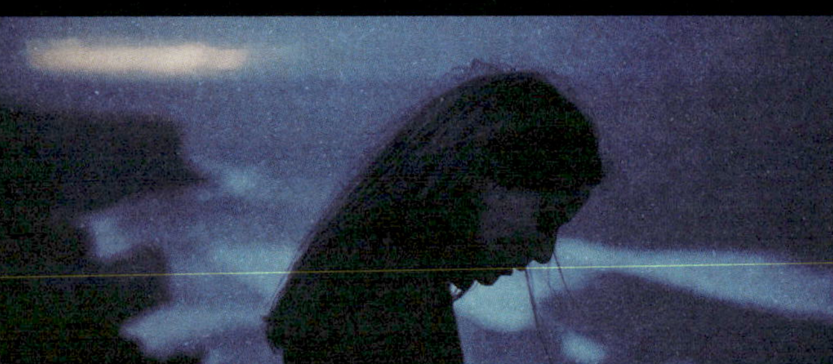 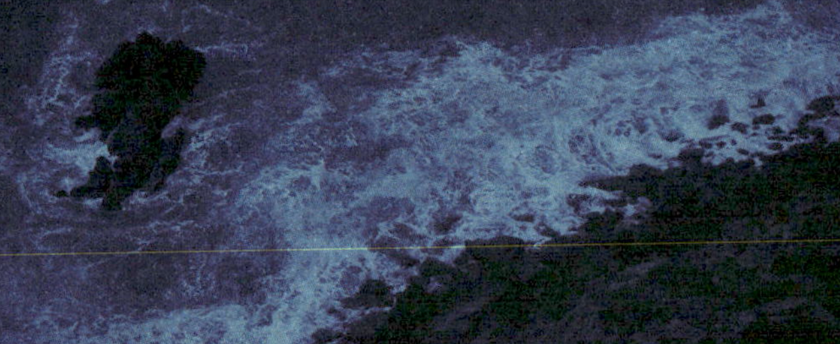 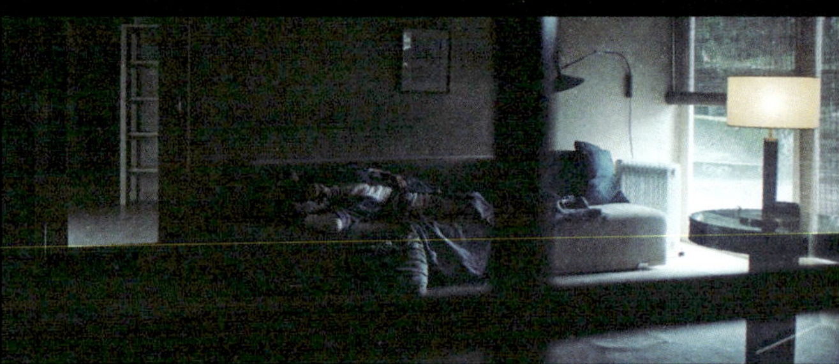

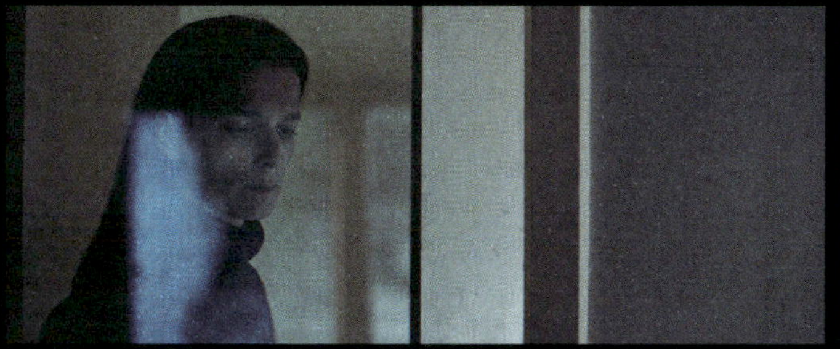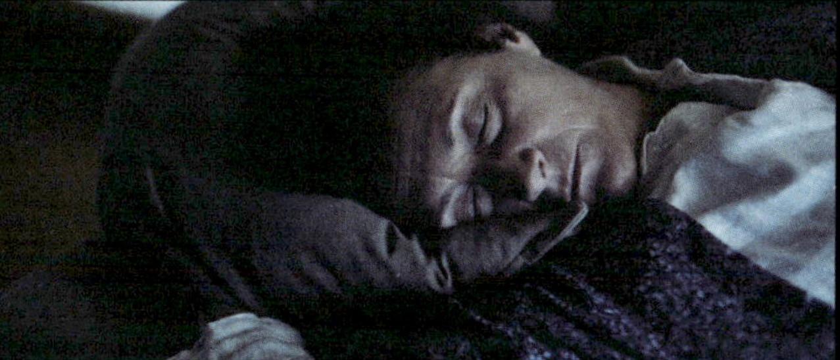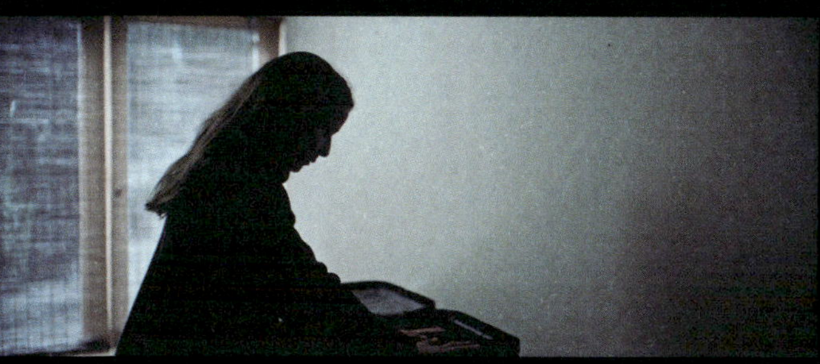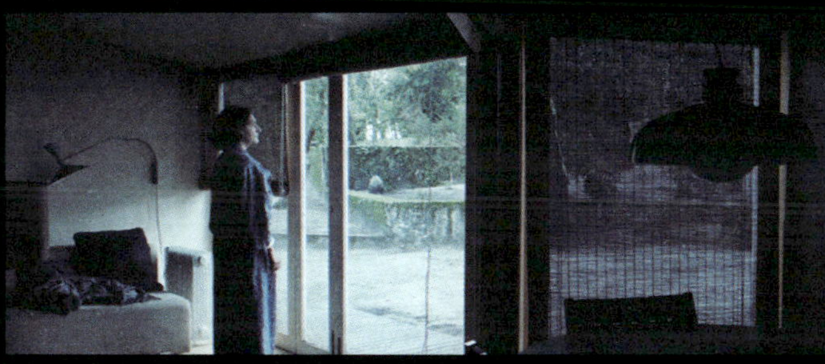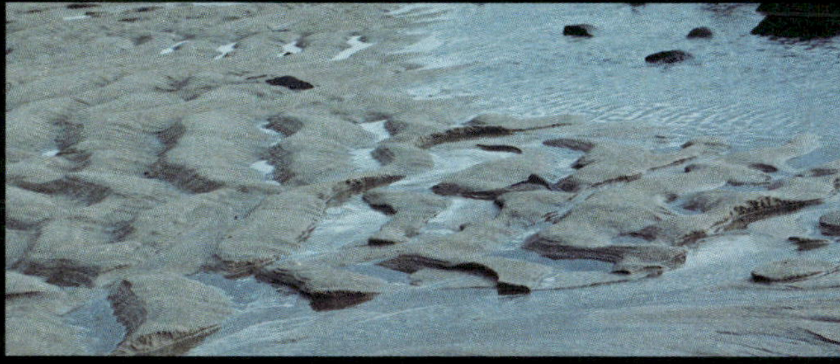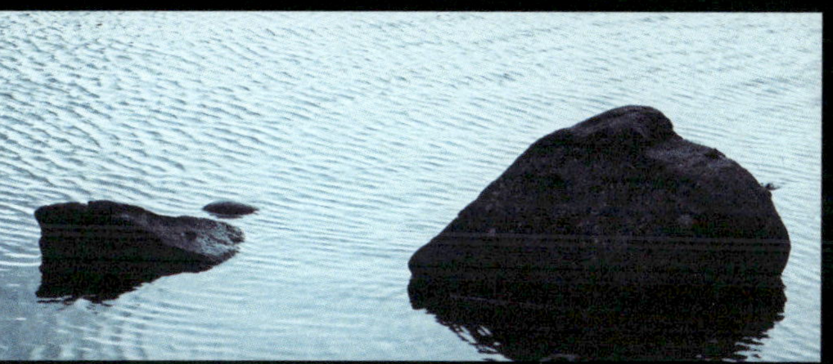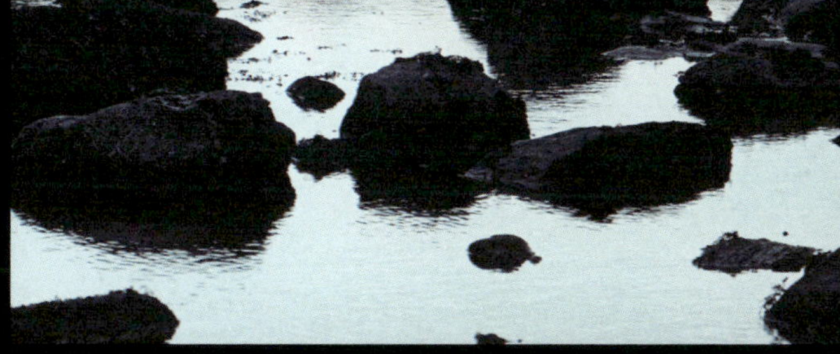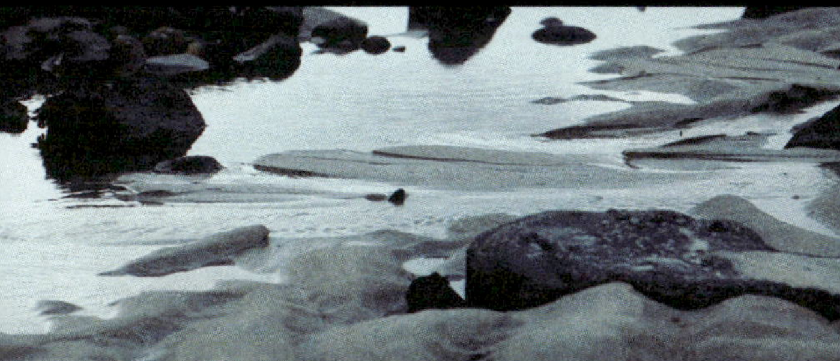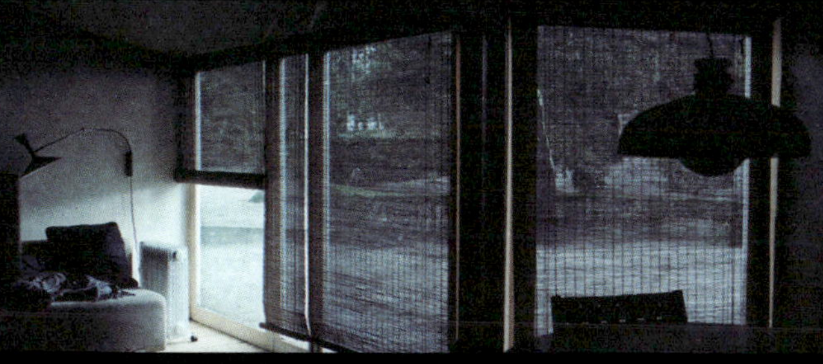

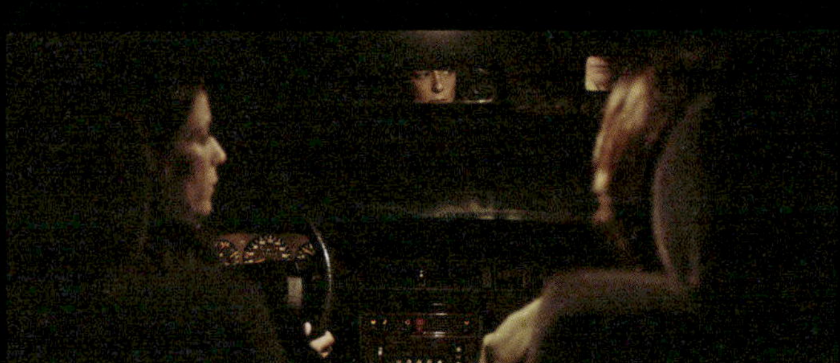
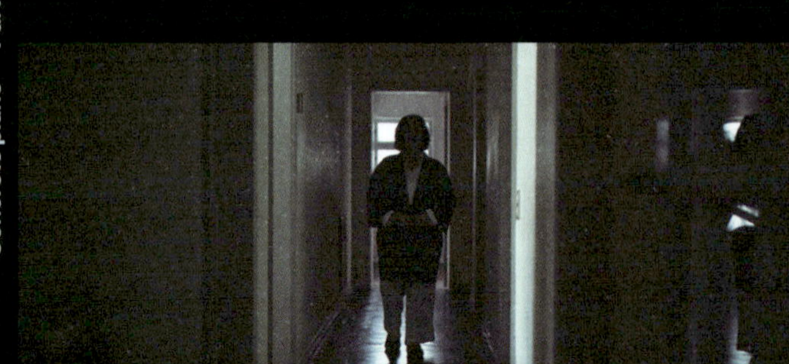

Concrete plane — Part III

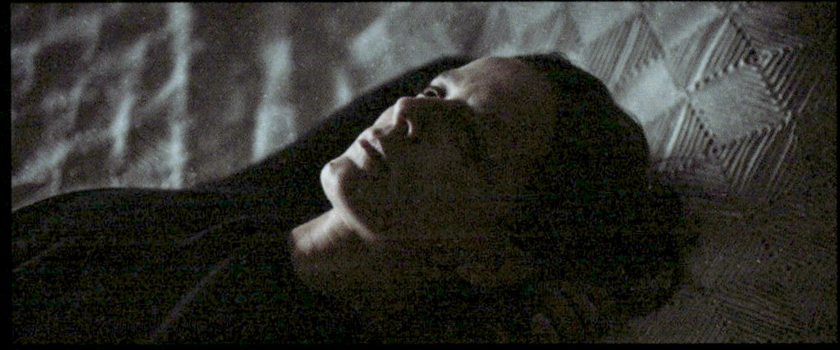
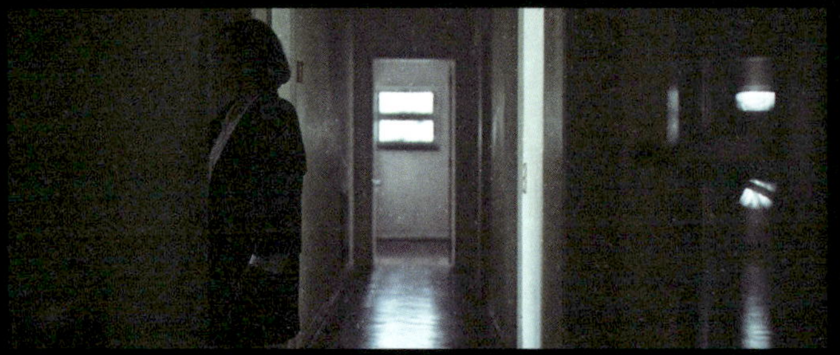

Abstract plane — Act III

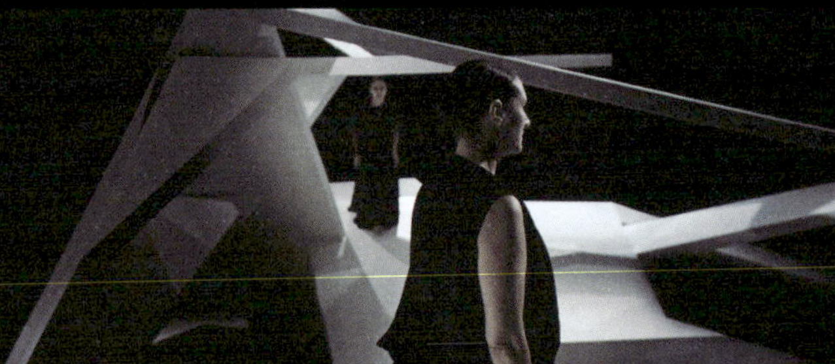
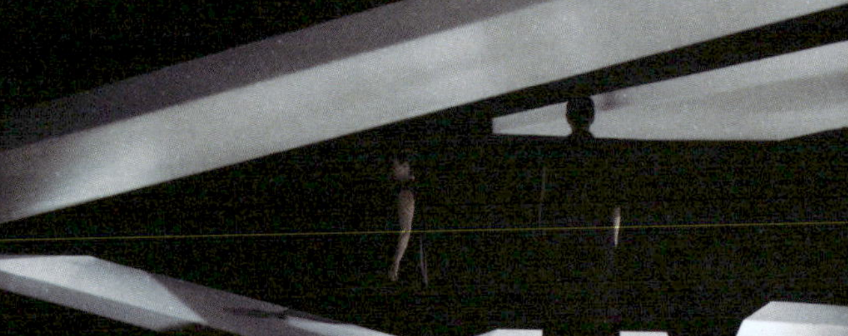
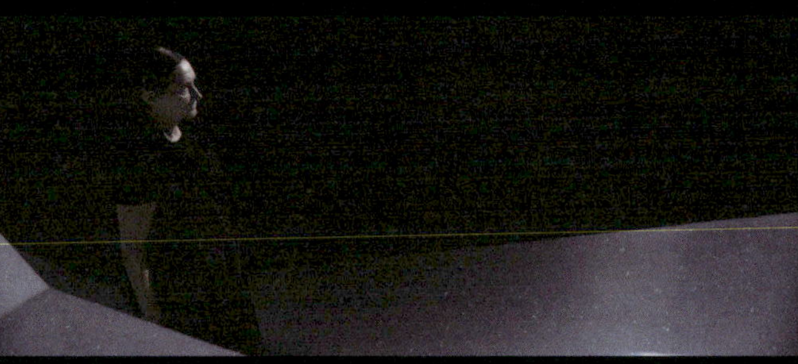

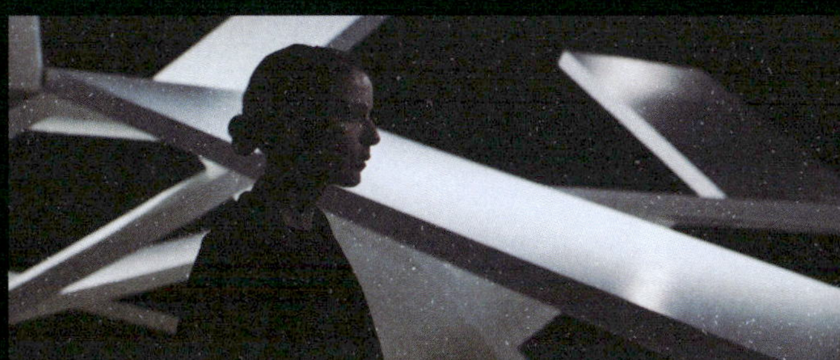

Irma:
The shift of the horizon from the earth to air conveys a progressive dissolution of the entire system of individualization, measurement, and location that makes the earth a habitable political space.

Carmo:
Extinction in the context of the great death of the solar system. Every temple built upon human conquests will inevitably be buried beneath the ruins of the universe.

Irma:
Don't heal. Live with our evils.

Carmo:
The basis of this conflict, of this fracture between the world and my spirit, what beyond consciousness do I have of it?

Irma:
None of the conflicts are solved, but all have been transfigured.

Carmo:
Revolution. Eternal movement, irresistible and repetitive of the celestial bodies. Every revolt, returns and revolts it is nostalgia for innocence. Appeal to being.

Irma:
Take up arms and assume full culpability, the crime of violence. Nostalgia ended up...
Now, victory is a thin and obviously provisional cover, under which the processes of disintegration continue unchecked, unable of replacing stability with chaos.

Carmo:
Only those who know freedom from need can fully appreciate inner freedom from fear, and only those who are free from both, need and fear, are able to conceive a passion for the freedom of the other. Where am I?

Irma:
Who asks? The one who sleeps or the one who awakens? Yes, sleep is total absence... I'm lost...I'm no longer there. No one is here anymore, except someone. The sleep of reason generates monsters. Monstrations. Demonstrations that reason can infinitely surpass itself even in sovereign unreason. Something, yes, sovereignty that is nothing, something out of nowhere where we come from and where we return to. Only a sleep...where we come from and where we return to.

Carmo:
A large black sun falls over my life.
Silence. Silence.

Irma:
Something happens inside.
Inside what?
Not inside. Not outside.
There is not.
Not within what countries are not, neither nations, nor walls.
Irreparably something has no place.

Carmo:
No thing returns to nothingness.
They all return, by aggre-disaggregation, to atoms. Not everything that seems to break-die completely perishes, because nature forms one thing again from another and it doesn't allow anything to be generated, except with the aid of the death of something else. Death is not a reign of terror.

Irma:
Create order from chaos and return to randomness. Atopy.

Carmo:
Past waltz. Embrace failure and complete incomplete revolutions.
Rethink the world.
Do it again.

Irma:
The moment of collapse is also a moment of beauty and emancipation.

Carmo:
Swallow fear, digest it and transform it into something else.

Irma:
Who will populate, this time, the in-between, the passage, the span between the nations. The nomad proletariat. The migrant brothers. The terrestrials. The homeless. Those whose community is the absence of community.

Carmo:
Another cosmology. An infinite
number of outsides of which the
universe is composed.

Irma:
Anthropological revolution.
A politic of existence that…

Carmo:
Choose a side, adopt an ethical
stance that refuses to put
all things on the same level.
Opposed to everything that
makes life impossible.

Irma:
One day, she said she gave me a home. It's true.
I didn't believe it. I never felt at home anywhere.
We cannot throw it away, nor free ourselves from what conditions
us. We can accept. Inevitable death, love life as mortals.

Carmo:
In a clearing, by the light of candles and oil lamps people drank
and spoke. All of a sudden, there was the sound of thunder. And out
of the dark wilderness an elephant emerged. An immense animal.
Silent. An elephant away from the herd is unpredictable.

Carmo:
We were all paralyzed. The elephant also stopped. Then it began to
walk between the tables. It shook its head. It didn't seem to have
made a decision yet. At a certain point, I crossed his gaze. It looked
at us attentively. In his eyes there was an enormous, unshakable
sadness.

Irma:
Chaos is supposed to be what
we fear the most, but I have to
believe it might be what we most
desire.

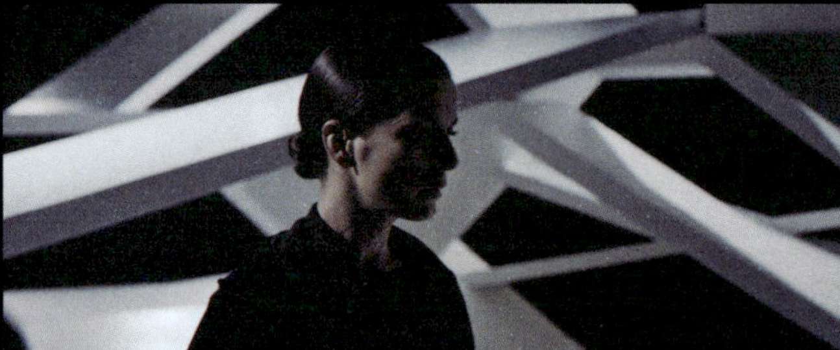

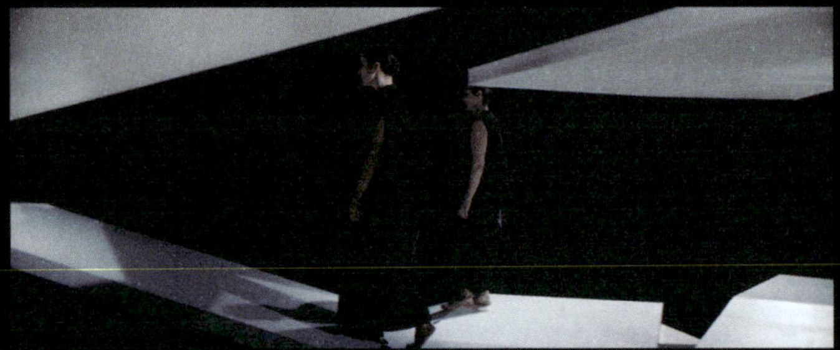

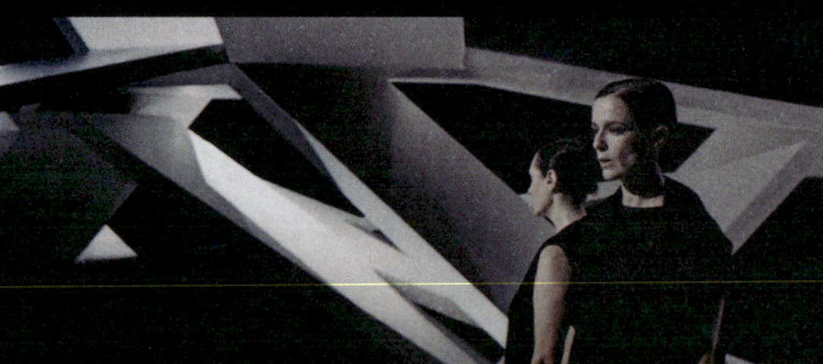

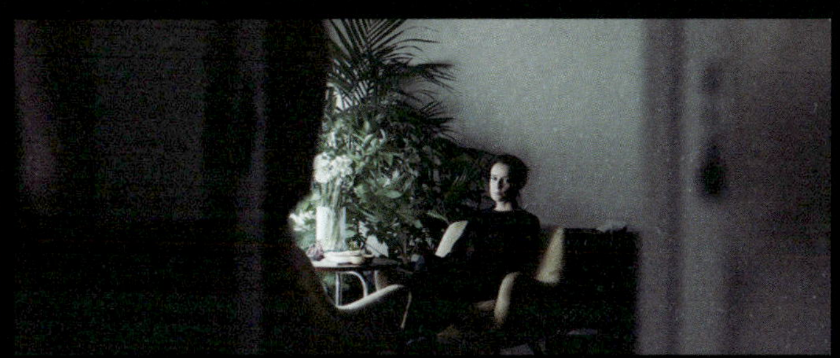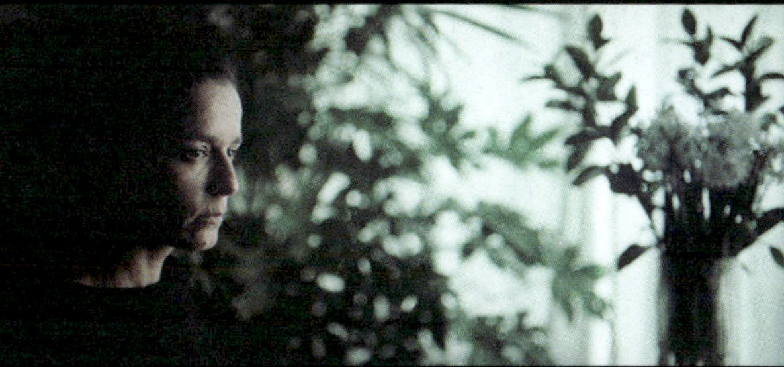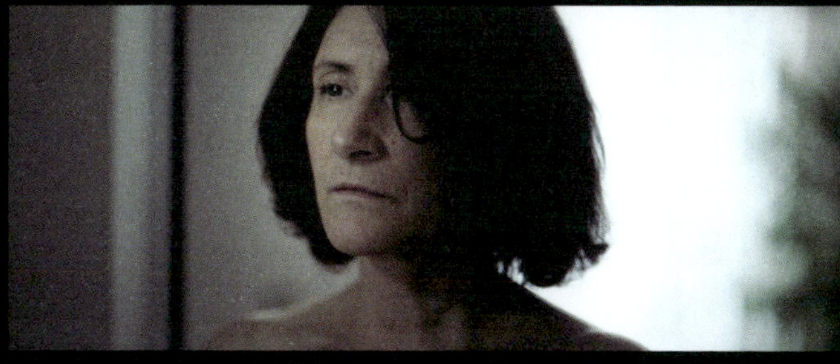

Irma:
I don't know what you expect to see.

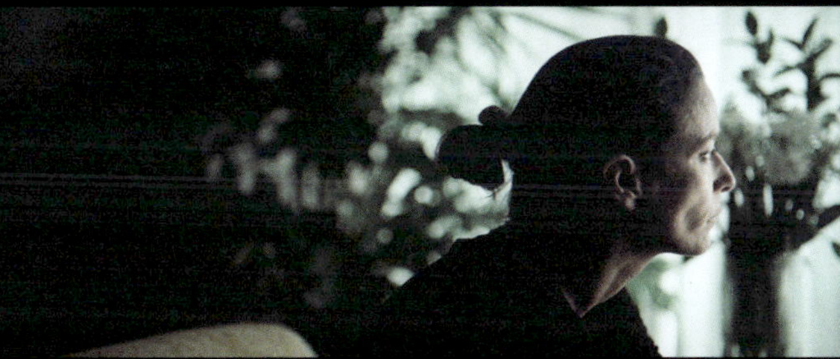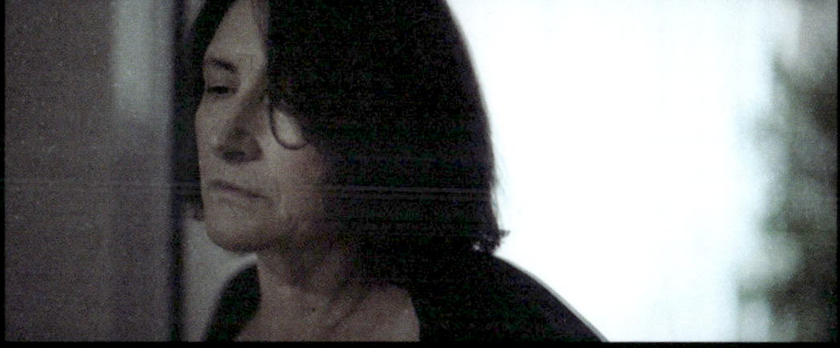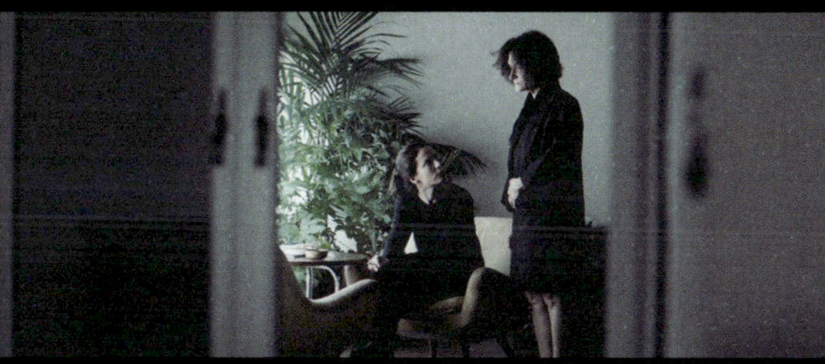

Irma:
You're still a beautiful woman.

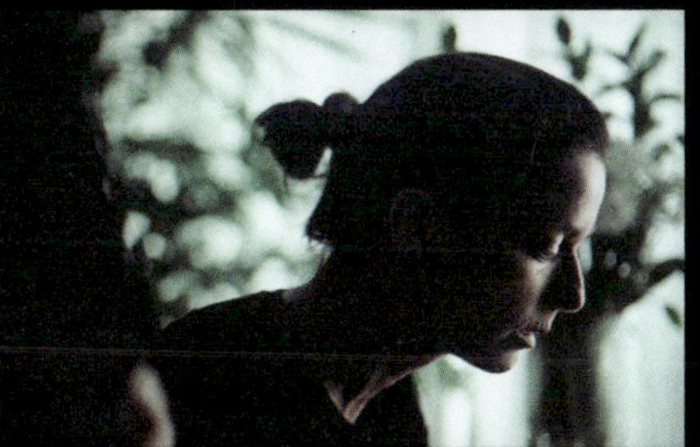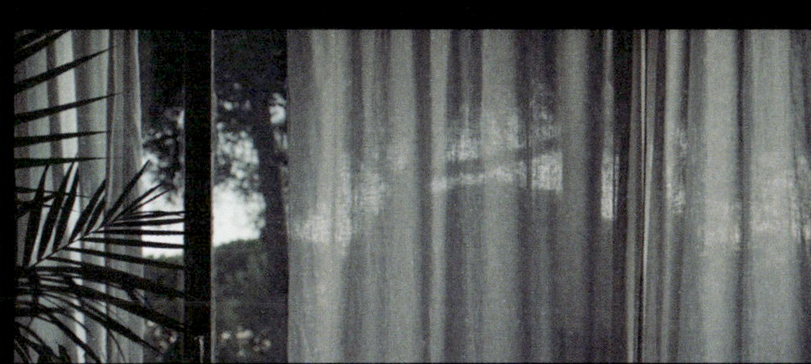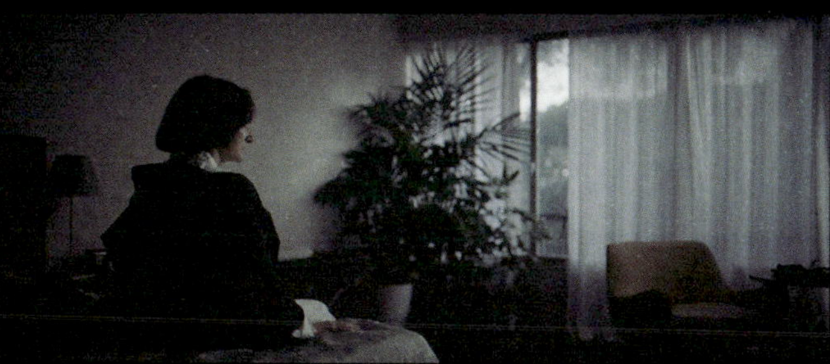

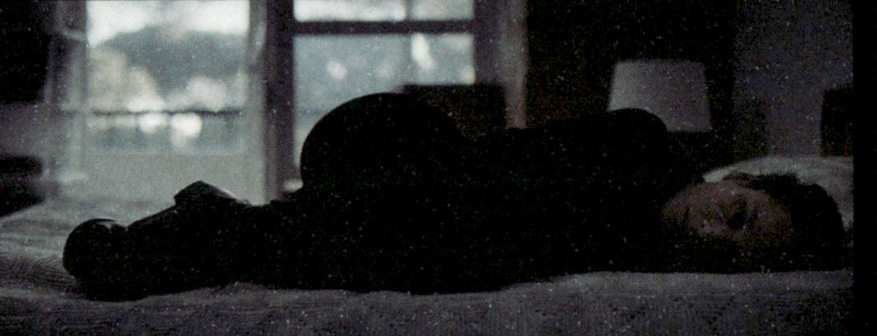 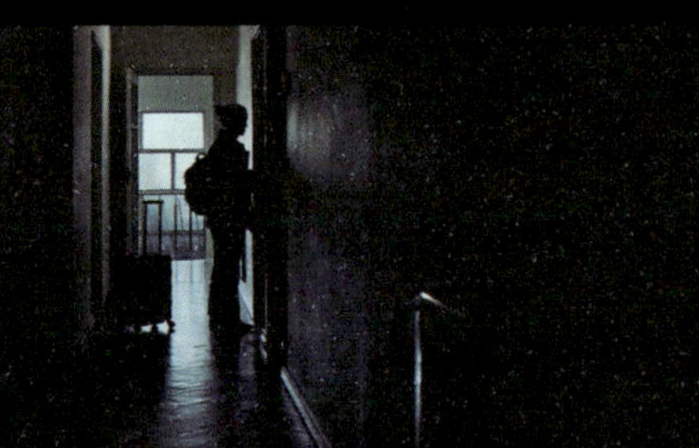 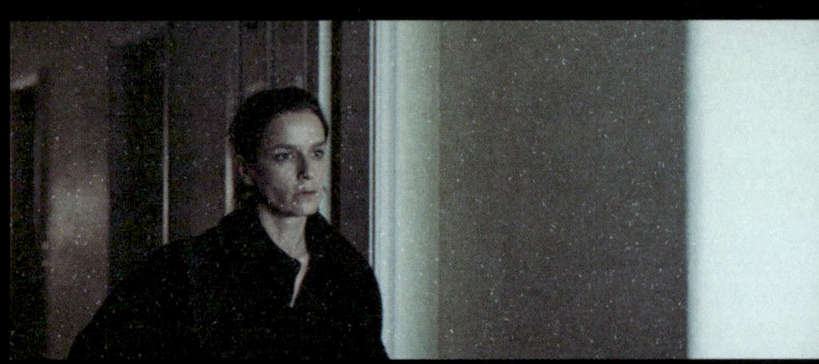

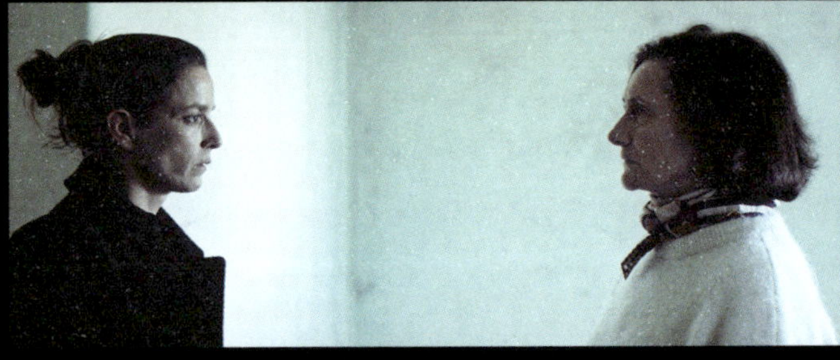 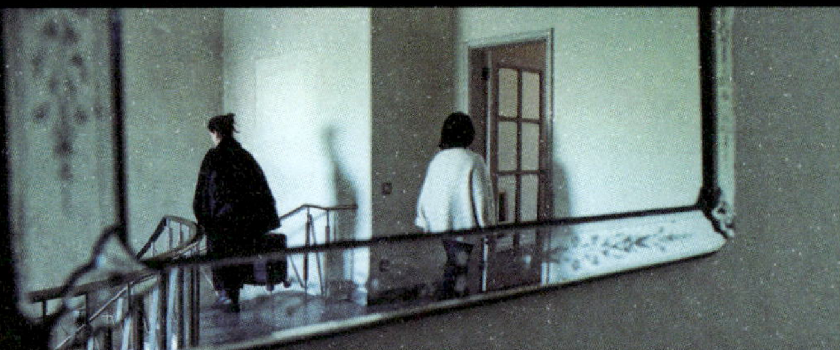 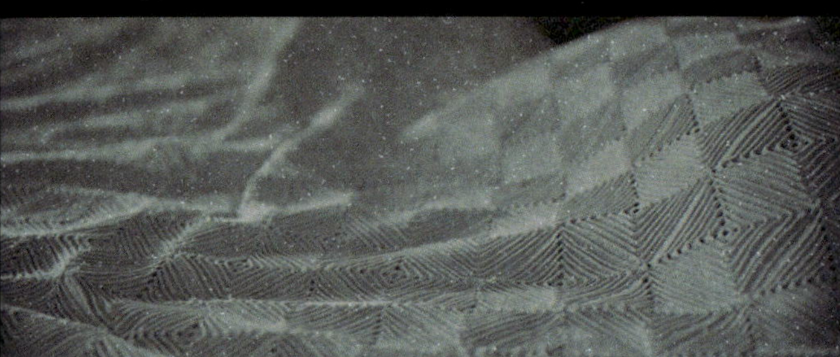

 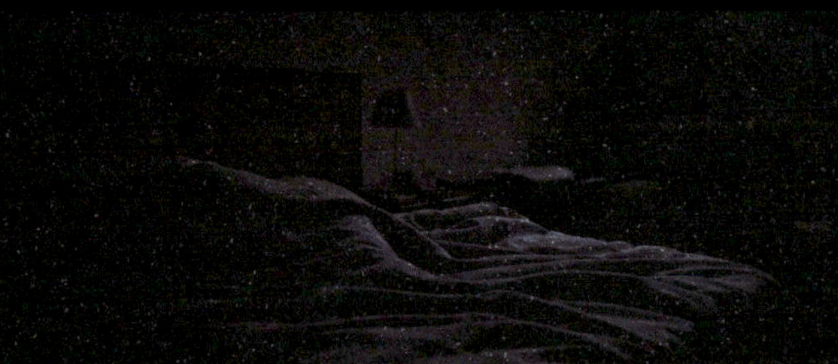 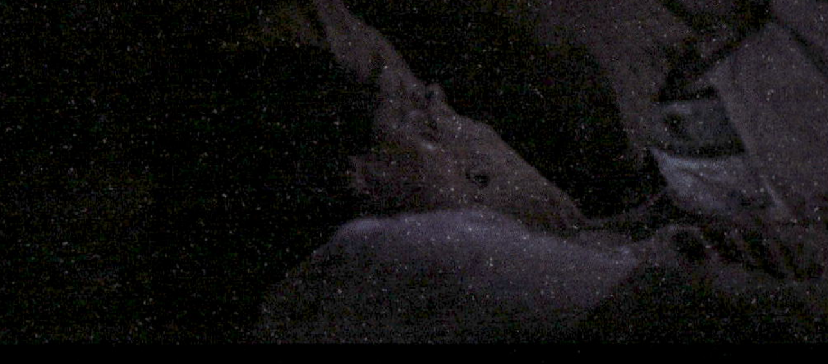

Abstract plane – Closing

Irma:
Another place.
Let it not be her.
Another place.

Carmo:
I want to have my eyes open
so I can close them.
I don't want to miss anything
that happens around me.
Another place.